D1371068

THE
MISCHIEF
-MAKER'S
HANDBOOK

This book is lovingingly dedicated to Beryl, Dennis,
Roger, Minnie, Mickey, Foxy, Buster, Lord Marmaduke
of Bunkerton, and all my other childhood chums,
not forgetting Beddy and Dann the Man.

LAURENCE KING

First published in 2020 by
Laurence King Publishing Ltd
361–373 City Road
London EC1V 1LR
United Kingdom
Tel: +44 20 7841 6900
E-mail: enquiries@laurenceking.com
www.laurenceking.com

Text © 2020 Mike Barfield
Illustrations © 2020 Jan Buchczik

Mike Barfield has asserted his right under
the Copyright, Design and Patents Act 1988 to
be identified as the Author of this Work.

A catalogue record for this book is available
from the British Library.

ISBN: 978-1-78627-551-6

Printed in China

Laurence King Publishing is committed
to ethical and sustainable production.
We are proud participants in The Book Chain Project ®
bookchainproject.com

**BOOK
CHAIN
PROJECT**

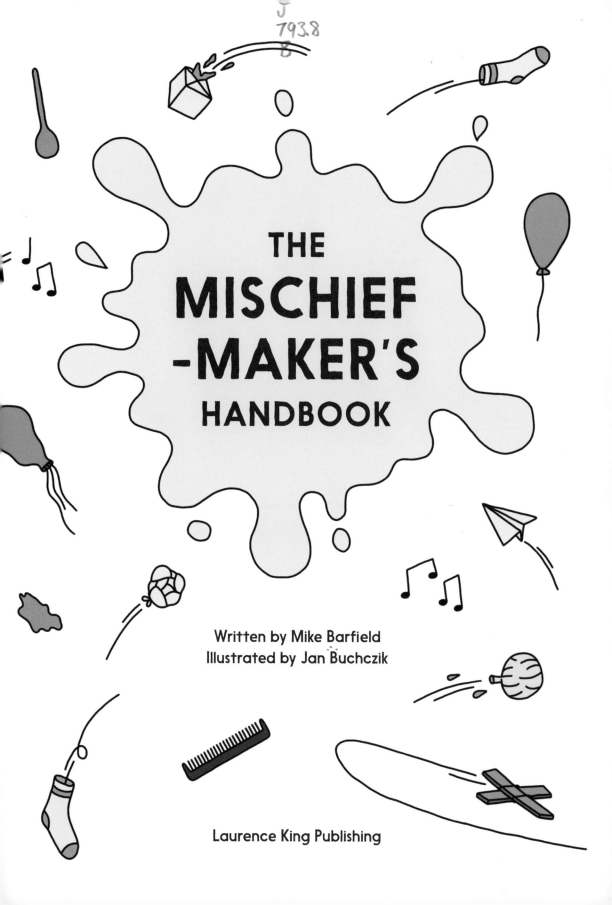

THE
MISCHIEF
-MAKER'S
HANDBOOK

Written by Mike Barfield
Illustrated by Jan Buchczik

Laurence King Publishing

CONTENTS

Answers 90

DO NOT READ THIS BOOK!

DO NOT read this book if you **DON'T** want to become any of the following:

- a Giant of Jokery
- a Pharaoh of Foolery
- the Dude of Rude
- the Tsar of Zaniness
- the President of Prankery
- the world's number one Nuisance Ninja!

DO NOT make any of the prank-tastic practical jokes it contains.

DO NOT attempt to repeat any of the amazingly annoying gags.

Close the covers and put it down immediately.

Even though almost all the things in this book will make grown-ups groan, teachers tremble, siblings sigh, and family and friends freak out, stop reading immediately!

WE REPEAT—DO NOT READ THIS BOOK!

WHAT, YOU'RE STILL HERE?

Great, then let's kick off the tricks and let the mischief begin...

YOU HAVE BEEN WARNED!

CHAPTER 1
MAKE A FAKE

There are some things like a whoopee cushion or fake poop that every joker needs in their collection. Don't worry if you can't get your hands on the real things because that's where these awesome fakes come in. They'll have you making mischief in no time!

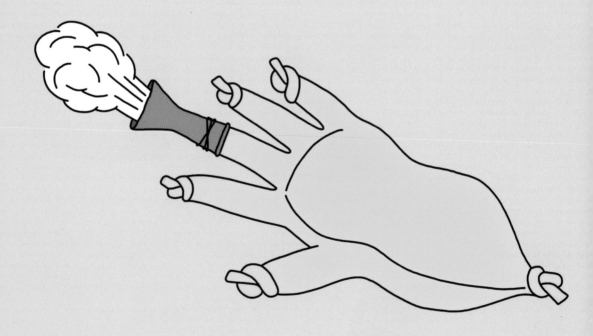

THRILLS AND SPILLS

White PVA glue is fantastic for making fake disgusting items.

You will need: • Plate • Plastic wrap • White PVA glue • Paints • Paintbrush • Cornflakes

 1

Cover a plate in plastic wrap. Pour white PVA glue onto the plastic wrap in the shape of the spill you are trying to fake.

 2

For a pretend milk spill, add white paint to the glue with a paintbrush. Toss in a few cornflakes and you have a breakfast-bowl calamity. Once the glue is dry, peel it off the plastic wrap and position.

3

Try different colors for other fakes. Add dark blue paint for an ink blot, green paint for bogies, red paint for blood stains or even white paint and a raisin for some pretty convincing bird poop. With a steady hand, you can even paint glue in fine lines to make fake spider's webs. Use your imagination!

Top tip! The glue may take a day or more to dry. Use the time to plot where you will place your bogus bogies and phony food spills!

HOW TO DO
TATTOOS

Want to make your parents panic and your friends envious?
These washable tattoos are the answer.

You will need: • Black fine-tip washable felt-tip pen • Washable felt-tip pens
(NOT permanent marker pens) • Tracing paper or parchment paper
• Roll-on deodorant, the type with a big ball at the end (if possible, use
a deodorant that is hypoallergenic so that it doesn't make your skin itchy)

①

For this pirate-style prankery, begin by
drawing a design on a piece of tracing
paper or parchment paper. Be creative!
Draw the outline first, with the fine-tip
black pen, and then color it in with the
other pens.

②

Roll a thin layer of deodorant over the
whole area of your skin where you
want your tattoo to be. (Note: Don't
do this on your face, near your eyes,
or anywhere you have a cut or a graze.)

Top tip! Your tattoo will print onto your skin in reverse, so you need to flip your image
and any writing you include. You can check if your design will print correctly by looking
at its reflection in a mirror.

③

Quickly, before the deodorant dries, slap your tattoo on top, ink-side down. Hold it firmly in place against your skin, but try not to move it or it may smudge. Wait a minute or so, then carefully peel off the paper.

④

A colorful tattoo image should be left behind. Some combinations of pens and deodorants work better than others, so try experimenting. Now frighten your family by showing them your new ink!

⑤ Have a go at designing all sorts of tattoos. Here are some ideas to get you started:

Top tip! When you get bored with it, you should be able to gently wash your tattoo off using soap and water. See you around, tattoo!

POOP IT OAT!

Make your own dodgy dog poop!
Fake dog poop is known to professional pranksters as "Naughty Fidos."

You will need: • Apron or old top • Large bowl • Oatmeal • White PVA glue • Plate
• Brown paint • Paintbrush

WARNING!
As you'll see below, making your own fake dog poop is a dirty job (literally); but someone's got to do it!

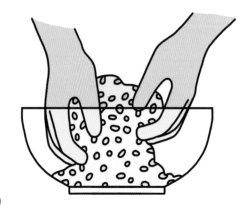

①

Put on an apron or an old top because things can get very messy. In a large bowl, mix together a handful of oatmeal and a dollop of PVA glue. It should form a sticky, stiff paste.

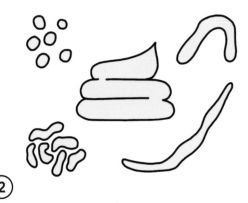

②

Using your hands, shape the mixture into a realistic poop shape. This could be a monster dog-log, curly, tapered, or lots of little round balls. You decide. Try to make the surface of your pretend poop as smooth as possible.

③

Next, leave it on a clean plate to dry. Your imitation poop may take several days to dry thoroughly. Keep it somewhere warm and turn it occasionally. When it is fully dry, paint your poop with several coats of brown paint to make it totally poop-tastic!

(4)

Now all you have to do is decide where to plant your deceptive dog poop. Will it be...

...here?

...here?

...or here?

Top tip! To really turn stomachs, pop your fake poop into an unused dog-poop disposal bag and stow it in a pocket. Take it out later when you are with your friends and ask them innocently: "Do you want to see what I found in the park today? It's a beauty. I'm going to add it to my collection." Then untie the bag and proudly display your homemade Naughty Fido.

WHOOP IT UP

Whoopee cushions are pretty much the most fun you can have sitting down.

You will need: • Strip of paper, about 2½ inches wide and 12 inches long • Pencil • Glue stick • Balloon • Scissors • Large rubber glove • Several rubber bands • Car wash sponge

1. Start by making your fart whistle. Wind the paper tightly around the pencil to make a paper tube. Use a glue stick to stick down the end of the paper strip so it doesn't unwind, and then slide out the pencil.

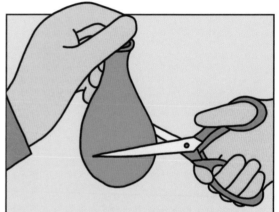

2. If you're using a round balloon, carefully cut across the rubber at its widest point with your scissors. For a sausage-shaped balloon, cut across the balloon at the opposite end from the mouthpiece.

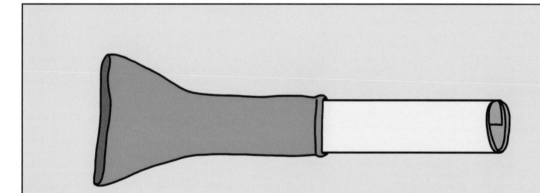

3. Insert the paper tube into the neck of the balloon, leaving as much balloon to hang free beyond the tube as possible. This gives you a wetter, richer fart noise. If the balloon doesn't cling tightly around the tube, secure it with a small rubber band. Blow the whistle and hear a fart!

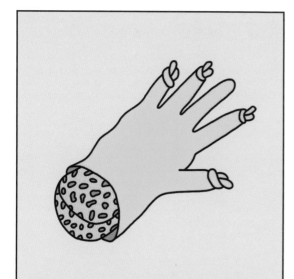

4. Now for your cushion! Tie a knot in each finger and thumb of the glove (or seal them off using rubber bands), except the middle finger. Knotting the fingers forces the air through the fart whistle. Stuff the sponge inside the glove until it is entirely covered and fits snugly inside.

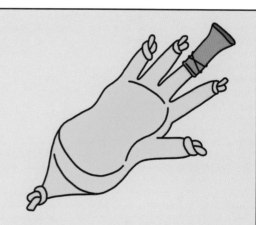

5. If there is enough spare glove, stretch it and knot the glove closed or seal using a rubber band. The sponge makes your parp cushion self-inflating. Now, carefully cut off the tip of the middle finger, then insert your fart whistle and seal it tightly with a rubber band. Give it a practice squeeze. It should fart nicely. If not, check all the seals to make sure air isn't escaping in the wrong places.

6. Place your whoopee cushion on a seat under a comfy cushion. Hard chairs work better than soft ones. Invite a victim to take the weight off their legs. Thrrrrrrpppp!

THE X-RAY-O-MATIC

X-ray specs are a huge joke-shop bestseller. Sadly, they don't actually work. However, nobody else needs to know that, and you can have great fun fooling your friends into thinking you own an X-ray machine.

You will need: • Stiff card • Scissors • Ruler • Pencil • Bird feather (craft stores sell colored feathers perfect for the part) • Scotch tape • Coloring pens or pencils

①

Carefully cut two pieces of stiff card into magnifying-glass shapes, complete with handles. In the very center of both, make a neat hole with a sharp pencil, about ⅜ inches wide.

②

Make a cut along the stem of the feather, right next to the stem, and then pull away a small piece of the feather.

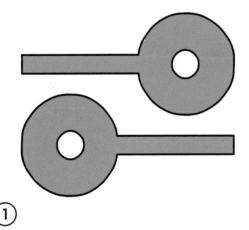

③

Place the piece of feather over the top of the hole in one of the magnifying-glass shapes. Use Scotch tape to attach in place.

④

Cover with the second magnifying-glass shape and join together with Scotch tape. Draw mystic symbols on your magnifying glass to add to the effect.

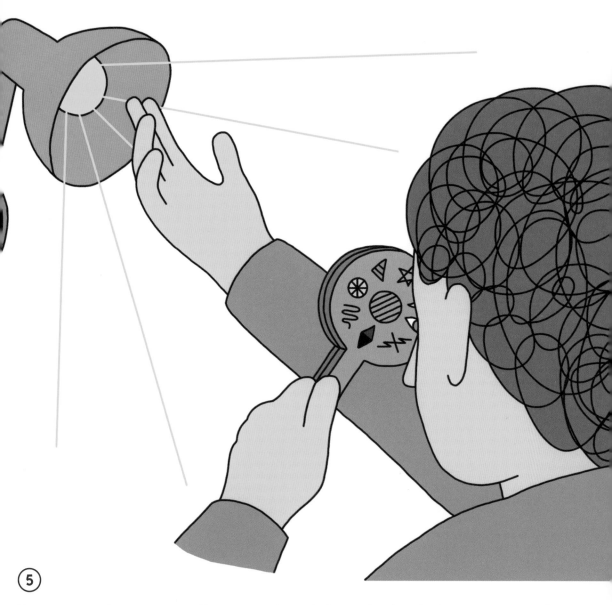

(5)

Now you are ready to try out your X-ray-o-matic! It works best on hands, so hold one hand up, at arm's length, in front of a bright light (not the sun). Take your X-ray-o-matic in the other hand, and look through the hole at the hand in front of the light. You should see what appear to be the bones of your fingers inside phantom see-through flesh. Spooky!

Having impressed your friends, use your X-ray-o-matic to pretend you can also see what is in their pockets or even what they are thinking about. If they ask you to prove it, just refuse, saying you don't want to embarrass them. They will be infuriated!

Top tip! If the effect doesn't seem to work at first, try rotating the X-ray-o-matic to a different angle, as it all depends on how light passes into your eye through the hidden piece of feather.

JUMPING FINGER
BANDAGE

This is a joke-shop classic.
Make a sympathetic friend jump (as well as your bandage)!

You will need: • Long strip of thin card • Scotch tape • Scissors • Small, thick rubber band
• White tissue paper or toilet paper • Red felt-tip pen

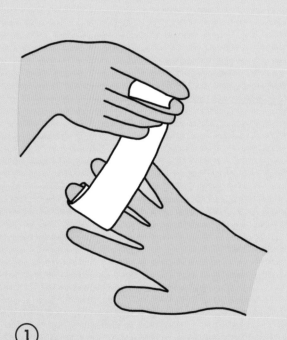

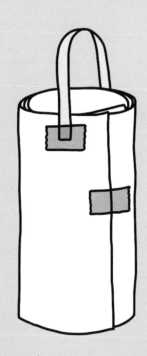

①

Begin by winding a long strip of thin card loosely around the top part of your middle finger to form a stiff tube. Tape it closed while in position, then take it off.

②

Next, carefully cut open a small, thick rubber band. Tape one end of the rubber band onto one side of the tube, then pass it over the open end of the tube and tape it in place on the other side. The rubber band needs to be just loose enough so it stretches when you push your finger into the tube. Check it does before moving on to the next stage.

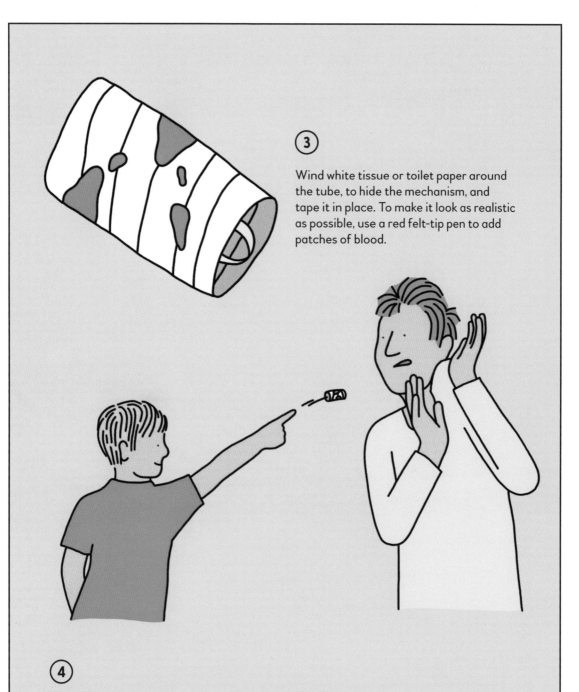

(3)
Wind white tissue or toilet paper around the tube, to hide the mechanism, and tape it in place. To make it look as realistic as possible, use a red felt-tip pen to add patches of blood.

(4)
Find someone to prank! Without them seeing, push the bandage onto one of your fingers, rubber-band end first so that your finger is poking the rubber band inside the tube. Hold the bandage in place with your other fingers. Look sad, then explain that you have hurt your finger and ask if they would kindly have a look at it for you. As their head comes close to your finger, let the bandage fly!

NAIL THROUGH
THE FINGER

One of the all-time greats! Try this timeless
trick on someone squeamish!

You will need: • Long, thin strip of card • Two flathead nails, about 1 inch long • Scotch tape
• Sticky tack or modeling clay • Toilet paper • Red felt-tip pen

WARNING!
Ask an adult to help you with this activity and handle the nails VERY carefully. If they have sharp
points, get a grown-up to blunt them with a metal file. You don't want to have a real accident!

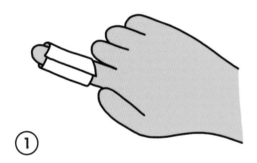

1

Begin by winding the card several times around a
finger so that your fingertip pokes out at one end.

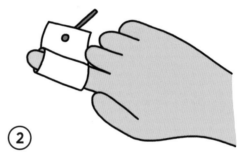

2

Unravel the end of the tube, and ask an adult to
carefully insert one of the nails through the paper,
near the end.

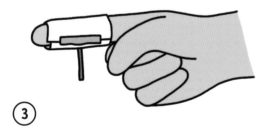

3

Wrap the card around your finger again so that
the flat head of the nail is inside the tube. Tape it
closed and take it off your finger.

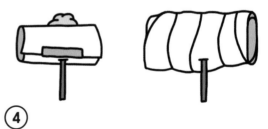

4

Place a small lump of sticky tack or modeling clay
on the other side of the tube, directly opposite the
nail. Now, starting at the lump of sticky tack, begin
winding toilet paper around the tube so it looks like
a bandage. Make the bandage nice and thick.

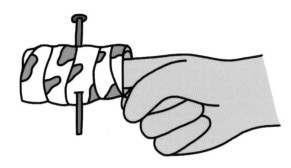

(5)

When you have done this (making sure that your finger is NOT in the tube!), ask an adult to carefully push the other nail into the concealed lump of sticky tack, so its point is sticking into the sticky tack and its head is poking out. It needs to line up with the first nail so it looks like one long nail has gone through your finger.

(6)

Finally, draw on some blood using a red felt-tip pen and slip your finger into the tube.

(7)

Now pull a pained face and go and find some people to disgust!

Top tip! Hide your bandage behind your back and innocently ask your friends: "Have you seen my strange fingernail?" Then whip it out. Shriek!

RATTLING GOOD FUN

Envelope rattlers are simple to make and a brilliant gag, especially on birthdays or other occasions when people receive cards or letters.

You will need: • Envelope • Thick card, corrugated is perfect • Pen or pencil • Scissors • Round mint with a hole in the middle • Two strong rubber bands

1. Lay the envelope on the card and draw round it. Then carefully cut out a rectangle from the card that is slightly smaller in height and width than the envelope.

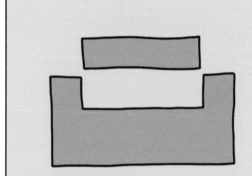

2. Next, carefully cut out a rectangular section from the top of the card about ¾ inches in from the edge on both sides.

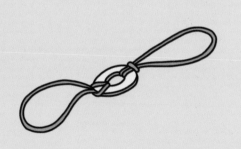

3. Thread a rubber band through the hole in the mint and then push one end of the rubber band through the loop on the other side of the rubber band (looping it through itself). This will attach it to the mint. Repeat on the other side of the mint.

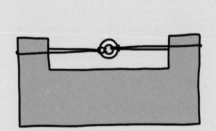

4. Loop the rubber bands around either end of the card so the mint hangs in the cut-out section. The bands should be lightly taut over the frame so they don't fall off.

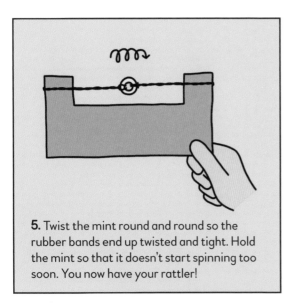

5. Twist the mint round and round so the rubber bands end up twisted and tight. Hold the mint so that it doesn't start spinning too soon. You now have your rattler!

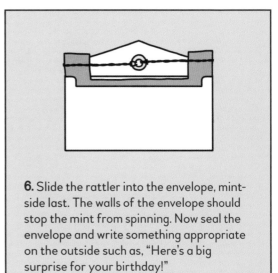

6. Slide the rattler into the envelope, mint-side last. The walls of the envelope should stop the mint from spinning. Now seal the envelope and write something appropriate on the outside such as, "Here's a big surprise for your birthday!"

7. Now for the fun! Hand the envelope to an unsuspecting victim. When they open it and begin to slide out the card, the freed mint should spin and make a fantastic rattling sound. TRRRRRRRRRRRRRRR!

Top tip! After startling your victim, ask politely: "Are you okay? Only, you look a bit, err, 'rattled.'"

CHAPTER 2
FLYING THINGS AND FLINGING THINGS

Missiles and mischief—how well they go
together! Just remember to be safe at all
times and to never fire your projectiles at
people's faces or at animals. (And don't throw
too hard—you could cause harm or injury.)

BALLOON BAZOOKA

This bad boy can toss paper pellets a seriously long way!

You will need: • Wide-mouthed plastic drinks bottle or milk carton • Scissors • Round balloon • Rubber band • Ball of paper

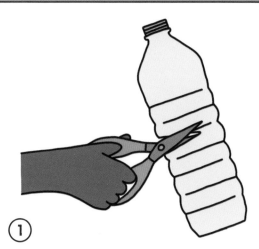

① Ask an adult to carefully cut a clean plastic water bottle, or milk carton, in half, keeping the top section.

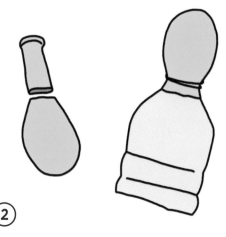

② Next, carefully cut the mouthpiece off a round balloon and discard. Take the main section of the balloon and stretch the open end over the neck of the bottle. Take care—the cut edge of the bottle may be jagged and sharp! Wrap a rubber band around the neck of the bottle to hold the balloon tightly in place. Done!

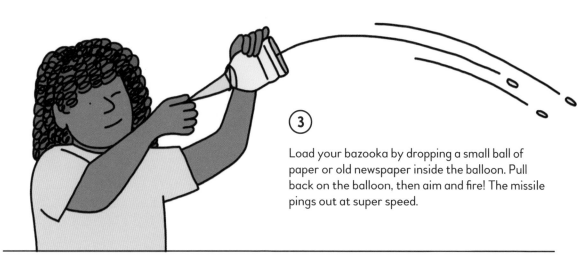

③ Load your bazooka by dropping a small ball of paper or old newspaper inside the balloon. Pull back on the balloon, then aim and fire! The missile pings out at super speed.

Top tip! Try firing several pellets at once.

WORLD'S SIMPLEST
STOMP ROCKET

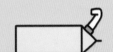 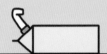

You will need: • Paper • Pencil • 32-fl-oz juice carton (dry inside)

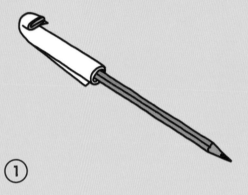

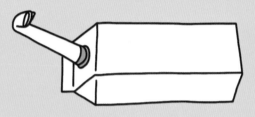

① Roll a small sheet of paper around a pencil to form a tube and twist one end closed.

② Remove the pencil and insert your paper tube at an angle into the spout of the carton.

③ Put the carton on the floor and then stomp on it. Wheeee!

Top tip! You can also use an empty juice carton to make the world's simplest whoopee cushion. Attach a fart whistle (see page 14) to the spout and hide under a cushion on a chair. Thrrrrp!

MAKE YOUR OWN
WATER BOMBS

Why buy bags full of teeny-weeny balloons, when you can easily make your own at home and give your friends a DIY dousing?!

You will need: • Plastic wrap • Cup or glass

① 1 Tear off a 12-inch length of plastic wrap and use it to line the inside of a wide-mouthed cup or glass. There should be lots of excess plastic wrap outside the rim of the cup. Slowly pour in cold water to partly fill the cup.

② 2 Bring together the corners of the plastic wrap and twist them together to form a sealed ball. Be careful—if you trap too much air or twist too tight, the water bomb will burst in your hand.

③ 3 Gently place the water bomb in the palm of your hand and find a good target. Ker-splash!

Top tip! Use super-wide plastic wrap to make a mega-bomb in a mixing bowl or saucepan.

THE PAPER
WATER BOMB

No one should be allowed to leave school until they know how to make one.

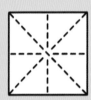

1. Take the Letter paper and fold one corner over to the opposite edge and crease. Carefully cut off the excess paper, then open it out and you will have a square.

2. Fold the top left corner of the square down to the bottom right corner. Unfold. The creases should make an "X" shape as shown.

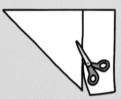

3. Fold in half, from top to bottom, to make a horizontal crease. Open out. Fold in half from left to right to make a vertical crease and open out.

4. Fold the left horizontal crease down to the vertical crease. Repeat on the right-hand side, then flatten to form a triangle (see above right for result).

5. Your triangle is now made up of two layers of paper. Fold up the bottom left corner of the top layer to the top of the triangle.

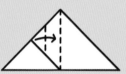

6. Fold the tip of the new triangle in toward the center crease (see above right for result).

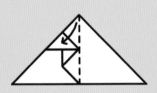

7. Fold down the top point of the top layer toward the left diagonal edge.

8. Fold this new triangle in half toward the middle.

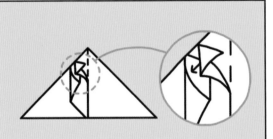

9. Lift the triangle up and tuck it into the small pocket in the triangle underneath.

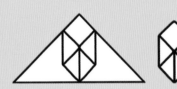

10. Repeat steps 5 to 9 for the right-hand side (see above left for result). Then turn over and repeat steps 5 to 9 on both sides (see above right for result).

11. Fold the top point down to center. Unfold. Repeat with the bottom point. Then flip over and repeat on the other side. Slide your fingers inbetween the folds on each edge to form an "X" shape.

12. Now, holding the paper in one hand, take the pencil and push it into the hole at top to enlarge it. Remove the pencil and blow into the hole to inflate the paper into a cube.

13. Fill with water and choose a target. Just don't leave it too long, or it will go soggy and soak you!

CARDBOARD BOOMERANG

You will need: • Thick cardboard • Scissors • Rubber bands • 12-inch rule

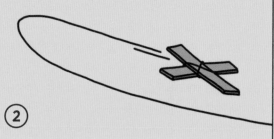

① Carefully cut two 12-inch-rule-sized strips of thick card. Place them in the form of a cross and join them together with rubber bands.

② Launch your boomerang outside! Throw it upward at a slight angle, with a flick of the wrist to set it spinning. With practice, it should loop upward and then return toward you.

MINI PAPER BOOMERANG

You will need: • Stiff paper or thin card • Scissors • Rule

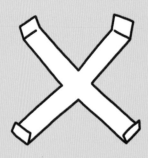

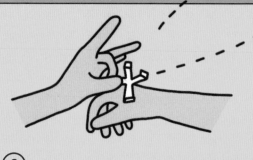

① Carefully cut out a 2-inch-wide, long-armed cross shape from a piece of stiff paper or thin card. Fold up the tips of the arms for extra stability.

② Place it on the back of one hand and flick it into the air with the other. It will spin and return, just like a real boomerang.

POPSTICK FRISBEE

Lucky you—for this you need to eat at least six popsicles!
Just for the sticks, of course. (Or you can use six wooden
drink stirrers from a coffee shop.)

You will need: • Six popsicle sticks or drink stirrers

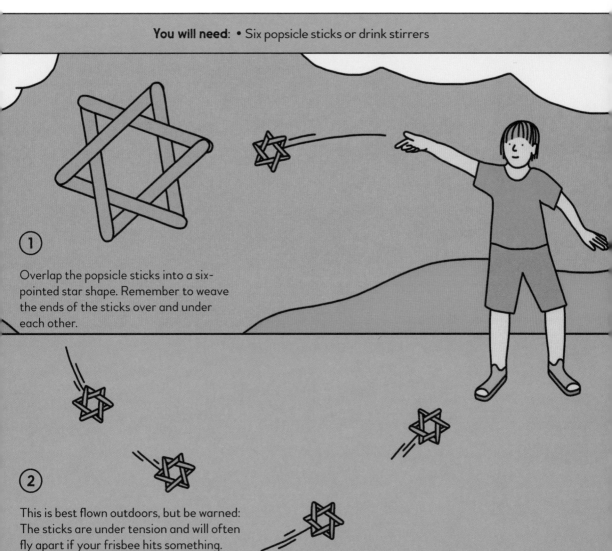

①

Overlap the popsicle sticks into a six-
pointed star shape. Remember to weave
the ends of the sticks over and under
each other.

②

This is best flown outdoors, but be warned:
The sticks are under tension and will often
fly apart if your frisbee hits something.

Top tip! Getting the sticks into place can be tricky, especially if they are short. You can make it easier by forming a triangle first and holding the ends in place with Scotch tape. Then weave the final three sticks into this triangle, and remove the tape. Soaking the sticks in warm water before you begin can make them easier to bend.

THE DART

This simple plane is a classroom classic.
Turn any rectangle of paper into a teacher-teasing feature.
Just don't get caught!

You will need: • Rectangular paper

(1)

Fold paper in half lengthwise, then open out, leaving a center-line crease.

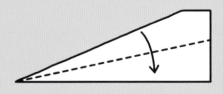

(2)

Fold the top two corners to the center-line crease.

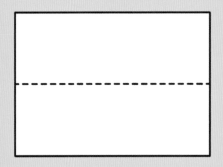

(3)

Now fold the diagonal edges you have just made into the center-line crease.

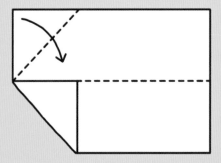

(4)

Fold in half. Then fold down the diagonal edges on both sides to make the wings.

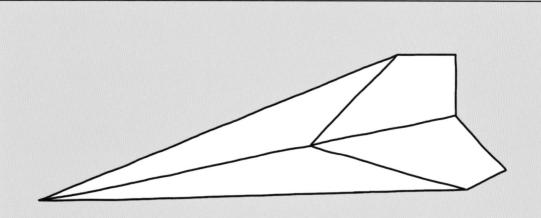

(5)

Done! A dart made with a piece of Letter paper will fly 30 feet easily. Launch it with a good strong steady throw, making sure no one is directly in its path.

Top tip! A smaller dart will often fly just as far and it is easier to hide. Try making different size darts to see which works best.

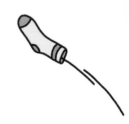

SOCKAPULT

This lets you sock it to 'em—literally!

You will need: • Piece of elastic, at least 3 feet long and 1 inch wide
• Clean socks and underwear

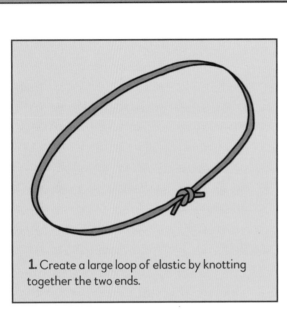

1. Create a large loop of elastic by knotting together the two ends.

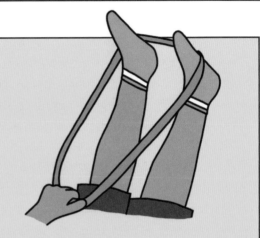

2. Loop the elastic over your feet and lie on your back, with your clean socks and underwear next to you.

3. Pull back on the middle of the elastic, then load up a sock (or a pair of pants!) and fire!

Top tip! You can get real distance by angling your feet up into the air or by using both sides of the elastic (to form a "U" shape hanging down from your feet).

SNOWBALLS IN SUMMER

Toilet paper is amazing stuff.
You can use it to make a pile of everlasting snowballs.

You will need: • Plastic wrap • Toilet paper

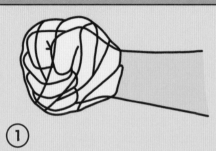 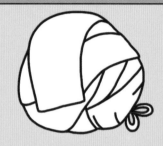

①

Begin by wrapping your fist in a large piece of plastic wrap then carefully slip out your hand. Now twist up the ends, trapping a big ball of air inside.

②

Gently wind clean white toilet paper around the plastic wrap until it is completely covered. Now lightly dampen the paper and wind a few further sheets round to soak up any excess water.

③

Repeat the process so you have lots of snowballs. Leave them somewhere warm to dry. This can take several days. Turn them occasionally so they dry all over. You can now toss snowballs at targets, even in a heatwave!

Top tip! Unlike the real things, these snowballs last forever. Just don't get them wet or have your victims squish them!

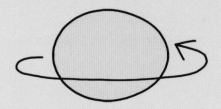

CHAPTER 3
SNEAKY SCIENCE

Not only is there an art to mischief-making,
there is a science too. All these silly pranks have
proper science behind them, but don't expect
to be hailed as another Einstein!

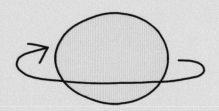

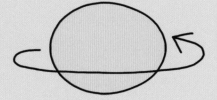

NOBBLED BOTTLE

This uses science to work its wicked trickery.

You will need: • Plastic water bottle • Pin

1

Fill a used plastic bottle with water and screw on the top. Then use a pin to pierce a few tiny holes in the side facing away from you. Air pressure will keep the water inside the bottle.

2

Find a good-natured victim and offer them the bottle, saying, "Would you like some water?"

3

As they reach for the bottle, squeeze it firmly—and thin jets of water will shoot out and soak them! Then run!

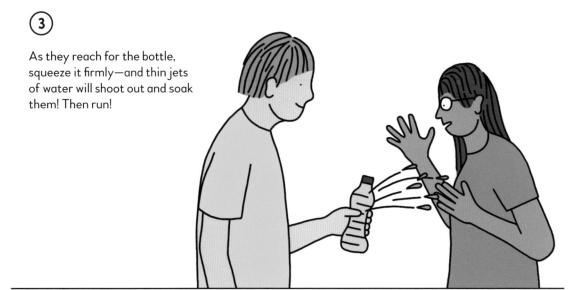

Top tip! Another form of this trick is to make a single pin hole in the small print on the bottle's label. Ask a victim if they can read what it says, then squeeze and squirt them with the water as they get close.

FART PUTTY

Fart putty is simply slime squished into a pot to produce disgusting noises. Slime is what chemists call a "polymer" and what mischief-makers call "fun!"

You will need: • Cup • Small bowl • Tablespoon • Laundry starch • Brown, green, and white paint • White PVA glue • Yogurt pot

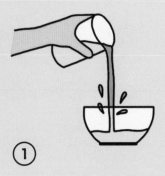

① Pour a cup of water into a small bowl.

② Add five tablespoons of laundry starch and stir until it looks like watery milk.

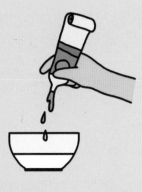

③ Add a dash of the brown paint to make it poop-colored! Or use the green and white paint to make snot-colored slime.

④ Squirt in the PVA glue. Mix the ingredients with your fingers to produce a nice sludgy lump of slime in the middle of the liquid. If you're not happy with the mix, simply add more starch or glue.

(5)

Next, fish out the slime from the bowl (you can pour away the remaining liquid), then squidge it into the bottom of the yogurt pot. Start pushing it around with your fingers—it needs to trap air, which then escapes around the sides—to produce horrible farty noises!

Top tip! Fart putty should keep for weeks if you cover it in plastic wrap and keep it in the refrigerator. However, handling it makes it dirty, so you'll eventually need to throw it away and make some fresh. Oh, and never eat it or put it in your mouth. It tastes disgusting.

INVISIBLE INK

Send secret messages to your friends with this easy invisible ink recipe.

You will need: • Knife • Lemon • Cup
• Cotton swab or paintbrush • Paper

> **IT'S NO JOKE!**
> During World War I, German spies living in Britain used fruit-juice inks to send each other hidden messages. When they were eventually captured, they became known as "The Lemon Juice Spies."

(1) Ask an adult to cut a lemon in half. Squeeze the two halves as firmly as you can over a cup to catch the juice, and then remove any seeds. Be careful you don't get any lemon juice in your eyes!

(2) Mix the lemon juice with water—half and half.

(3) Dip a cotton swab or paintbrush in your invisible ink and write a message, or draw a picture, on a piece of paper and let the paper dry.

(4) If you want, you can also fold and crumple the paper to disguise any crinkles caused by the ink wetting the surface.

(5)

To reveal the secret message, simply hold it up to a heat source, such as a hot radiator or light bulb. The heat causes chemicals in the ink to turn brown, enabling you to read what was written. You can even get a grown-up to iron it for you—provided you can trust them to keep it a secret!

Top tip! You can make other invisible inks using onion juice and even diluted milk!

EGG SPIN MAGIC

A seemingly magical trick that is actually simply science.

You will need: • Carton of six eggs • Saucepan

(1)

Ask an adult to hard boil one of the eggs for 7–10 minutes, and let it cool for a few hours.

(2)

Then place it back in the carton with the five raw eggs.

(3)

Now tell a friend to shuffle the six eggs around in the carton and say that you will be able to pick out the one that is cooked. Invite them to examine the eggs for marks—they won't find any.

(4)

Lay all six eggs on a smooth tabletop and start spinning them, one at a time. One by one, gently place a finger on each egg to stop it turning. The cooked egg will be the only one that doesn't start slowly spinning again after you have tried to stop it. The raw eggs continue to turn because their runny contents are still moving inside, even though the shell has been stopped.

(5)

If you wish to look dramatic, you can safely bash this egg with your hand without making too much mess.

Top tip! Don't get this wrong. It will be messy if you do!

CHAPTER 4
NOISY TOYS

"What noise annoys an oyster most? A noisy noise annoys an oyster most!" This well-known tongue-twister is true for humans too. The ability to be loud in a crowd, and get a noise out of anything to hand, is an essential element for would-be mayhem makers. Luckily there are many wonderful ways to bring fear to ears and get yourself heard.

BOOK HARMONICA

Turn every novel into a horror story with this nail-biting noise.

You will need: • Paperback book

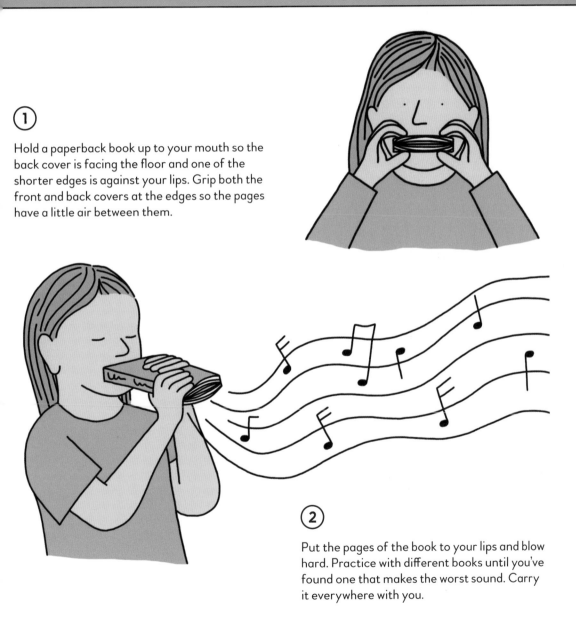

① Hold a paperback book up to your mouth so the back cover is facing the floor and one of the shorter edges is against your lips. Grip both the front and back covers at the edges so the pages have a little air between them.

② Put the pages of the book to your lips and blow hard. Practice with different books until you've found one that makes the worst sound. Carry it everywhere with you.

Top tip! A great way to break an awkward silence. Just say you were blowing away the dust!

THE DIDGERIDON'T

Similar to the ancient Australian musical instrument, the didgeridoo, except people won't want to hear you playing this one.

You will need: • Cardboard or plastic tube, about 24 inches long and 2 inches wide

IT'S NO JOKE!
The world record for playing a single note on a didgeridoo using one breath is just over 65 seconds.

① Practice a sloppy raspberry. Gently purse your lips, then stick your tongue out and blow.

② Next, place the tube to your lips and blow your sloppy raspberry down the pipe. Hit just the right note and it will produce a big booming noise.

③ Keep practicing until you can hold a note for a long time from just one breath. People will be amazed—or annoyed...

Top tip! Dedicated didgeridoo players learn a technique known as circular breathing. Just before they have exhaled all the air in their lungs, they breathe in more air through their nose. Try it!

TUBULAR TRUMPETRY

You will need: • Cardboard tube from plastic wrap or aluminum foil

① Practise a "dry" raspberry—the tongueless one that trumpeters use. Purse your lips tightly, leaving a small gap between them. Blow really hard so your lips vibrate.

② Next, try this down the tube. Keep blowing until you get the right note. Hit this and you can really have a blast!

SUPER-SQUEALER

You will need: • Strip of paper (no wider than the length of your fingers) • Scissors

① Fold the piece of paper in half, then carefully cut out a V-shaped notch from the fold. Then fold back a small section at both ends to make handles.

② Place the squealer between two fingers and blow hard. The noise is horrible!

Top tip! Experiment with adding an extra notch or two in the fold.

GLASS HARMONICA

An after-dinner, or restaurant, classic.

You will need: • Wine glasses

IT'S NO JOKE!
Giant glass harmonicas made up of a long row of turning glass bowls were played in orchestras over 200 years ago!

1. Ask permission from an adult to use a wine glass. Check there are no chips or sharp edges on the rim of the glass. Pour a small amount of cold water into the glass.

2. Dip a finger in and begin gently, but firmly, to rub your wet finger around the rim of the glass, holding the base carefully on a tabletop.

3. Get just the right speed and slipperiness, and the glass should begin to make a wonderful ringing sound.

4. You can vary the note by how much water you have in the glass. More water produces a lower note.

Top tip! Fill eight wine glasses with differing amounts of water and you can play a scale of notes and even actual music!

ICE POP HARMONICA

Making this wheezy wonder means you will need
to eat THREE popsicles—yum!

You will need: • Three popsicle sticks • Rubber band • Scotch tape

①

Stretch the rubber band lengthwise over
one of the popsicle sticks.

②

Place the other two popsicle sticks above
and below it to form a "popsicle stick and
rubber band sandwich." Wrap Scotch
tape around one end of the sandwich
to hold it together.

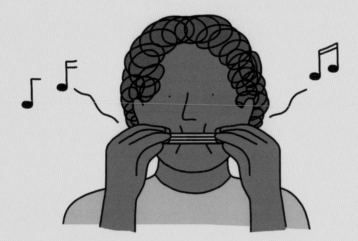

③

Now hold the harmonica gently at each end, bring it to your lips and blow. It should produce
a penetrating wheezy noise like a crying baby!

Top tip! You can vary the noise by pushing on the ends of the popsicle sticks so that
they bow apart slightly in the middle. Dogs go crazy for the sound!

THE BULLROARER

This ancient device is used for sending signals over long distances, meaning it has probably been annoying people on the planet for thousands of years. It produces a low whirring drone when you swing it slowly over your head.

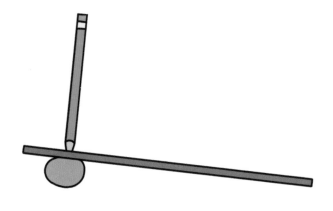

①

Carefully cut a strip of thick, strong cardboard, about 1 × 7 inches. Place a ball of modeling clay or sticky tack about 1 inch from one end. Turn the cardboard over and, using the sharp point of a pencil, pierce a hole through the cardboard and into the modeling clay or sticky tack. Remove the clay and pencil.

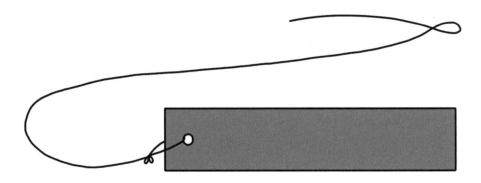

②

Pass the end of your thread through the hole and tie the two ends together, creating a loop. As you are going to be whirling this around your head, make sure the knot is really secure.

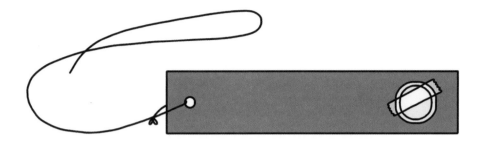

(3)

Next, tape a heavy coin (or more than one coin) to the opposite end of the card from the thread. Use plenty of tape to make sure it doesn't fly off. You don't want to be throwing your money away!

(4)

Now find a safe place outside, somewhere you won't hit anything or anyone. Twist up the thread on the bullroarer before beginning, then swing it in a circle either above or in front of you. Get the right speed and this should produce a low, throbbing hum.

Top tip! Try making bullroarers of different shapes and sizes. The thread needs to be thin and strong, or the card won't spin enough to generate noise.

COMB AND PAPER

The forerunner of the raspy kazoo, and just as annoying in the wrong hands (yours!).

You will need: • Hair comb—not one with a spikey handle • Tracing paper or parchment paper • Scissors

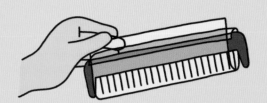

① Carefully cut a piece of tracing paper or parchment paper to the length of the comb and at least twice its width. Fold it lengthwise over the comb so the teeth lie along the fold.

② Holding the comb between the thumb and forefinger of each hand, bring it up to your lips, with the comb's teeth facing upward. With dry lips, begin to hum your favorite tune. As you do so, touch the paper on the side of the comb against your lips.

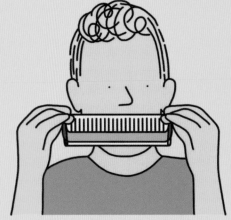

③ It may tickle a bit at first, but the vibrations of your lips should transfer to the paper to make a loud sound. Practice until you can get a satisfyingly awful sound every time.

SPOONEY SPOONS

Spoons aren't just good for eating ice cream, they can also make a percussion "instrument."

You will need: • Two matching metal spoons

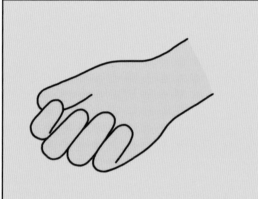

1. Form a loose fist with whichever hand you use for writing, and turn your fist so your palm is facing your stomach.

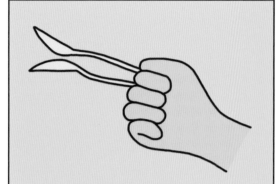

2. Insert the handle of a spoon between the thumb and forefinger. Turn the second spoon upside down and place it between your forefinger and middle finger so the backs of the spoons are almost touching.

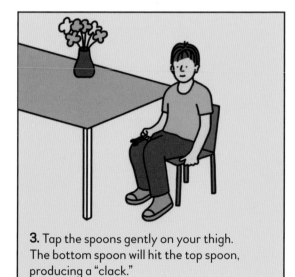

3. Tap the spoons gently on your thigh. The bottom spoon will hit the top spoon, producing a "clack."

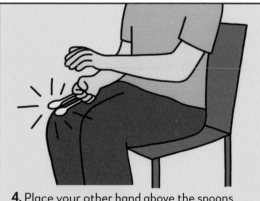

4. Place your other hand above the spoons and you can get another "clack" on the upstroke. Keep tapping until you get a rhythm going. You can also tap your spoons on your arms or head. Just don't knock yourself out!

Top tip! Professional players can make amazing sounds. Check some out on the Internet.

YOGURT-POT TELEPHONE

Make this yogurt-pot telephone so you can make mischievous
plans with your friends without grown-ups listening in.

You will need: • Two empty yogurt pots or paper cups
• Scissors • String, at least 6½ft long

①

Ask an adult to carefully use scissors to pierce a
hole in the bottom of each yogurt pot or cup.

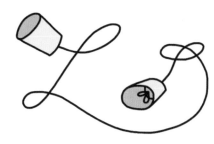

②

Push one end of your string through the hole in the
bottom of one cup and the other end through the
other cup. Then tie a knot at either end, which will
sit inside each pot and join the two together.

③

Get a friend to hold a pot up to their ear while you pull the line tight and speak into the pot. As long as the
line is tight, they'll be able to hear you.

Top tip! You can't both talk at the same time, so remember to say "over" when you have finished speaking.

DRINKING-STRAW CLARINET

♪ ♪ This traditional trick makes a wonderful beastly buzz. ♪ ♪

You will need: • Paper drinking straws • Scissors

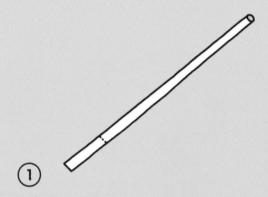

① Flatten the last half-inch or so at one end of a straw.

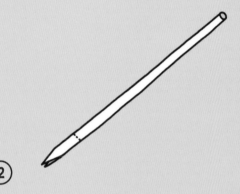

② Carefully use scissors to snip a diagonal section off either side of the flattened part of the straw.

③ Place the cut end of the straw in your mouth and blow firmly. The cut ends should vibrate to produce a reedy buzz. If it doesn't work at first, try trimming the end a little more.

Top tip! Different-length straws make different pitches. Try making several straws of different lengths and you should be able to blow an octave! To make your clarinet even louder, ask an adult to pierce a hole in the bottom of a yogurt pot or paper cup just big enough to insert the bottom end of your straw. Now when you blow, the buzz should be bigger!

THE PAPER BANGER

These can be quickly folded from a single sheet of A4 paper, so you can make lots in a flash. The noise of a bunch of bangers going off together is hugely amusing. Unless you're a snoozing grown-up.

You will need: • Letter paper

IT'S NO JOKE!
The record for the largest origami paper banger was set by Paul Jackson at University College, London, in 1980. He started with a sheet of paper 2.7m by 1.67m (8 feet 10 inches by 5 feet 6 inches), producing a banger over 1.5m (4 feet 11 inches) long, which actually worked. Bang on!

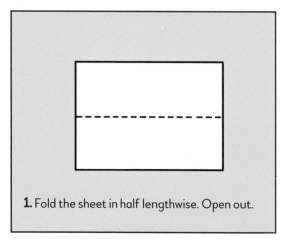

1. Fold the sheet in half lengthwise. Open out.

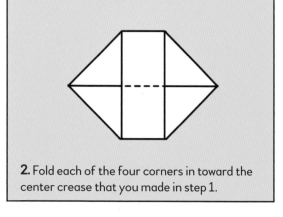

2. Fold each of the four corners in toward the center crease that you made in step 1.

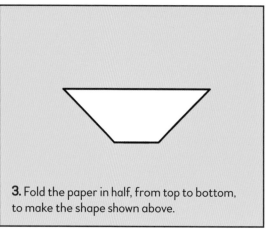

3. Fold the paper in half, from top to bottom, to make the shape shown above.

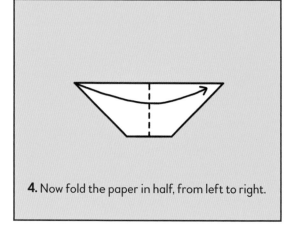

4. Now fold the paper in half, from left to right.

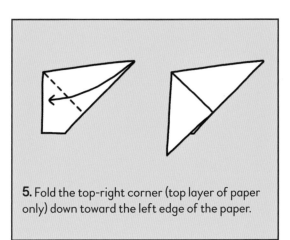

5. Fold the top-right corner (top layer of paper only) down toward the left edge of the paper.

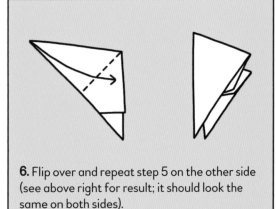

6. Flip over and repeat step 5 on the other side (see above right for result; it should look the same on both sides).

7. Hold the two bottom corners (see step 6) cock the banger upward, then bring it down as quickly as possible. Bang!

Top tip! You can make bangers from any rectangle of paper provided it is not too thick or stiff. Try making a banger using a single whole sheet of newspaper. The bang it produces can be so loud as to actually rip the paper!

BLOW YOUR TOP

Even if you aren't learning the recorder or flute,
you can still "delight" your family with loud shrill whistles.

You will need: • Glass bottle • Pen top

① Bring your lips level with the top of a glass bottle and gently blow across the top. It will often produce a lovely deep note, caused by a column of air vibrating inside it. Try filling the bottle in varying amounts to get different notes.

 ② Experiment with blowing across anything that comes to hand. Using the same technique you can produce much more piercing sounds from pen tops and other smaller tube-like objects that are closed at one end. (If the pen top has holes in both ends of the cap, cover one of them with your thumb to improve the sound.)

Top tip! A bicycle pump is fun to try—blow across the end of the pump and you can vary the pitch by moving the handle up and down!

SWANEE WHISTLE

Why not make your own paper Swanee whistle?

You will need: • Pencil (with a circular body, not hexagonal)
• Card or stiff paper • Scotch tape

(1)

Wind the paper or card tightly around the pencil several times to form a tube. Seal with Scotch tape so it doesn't come undone. Make sure you can still move the pencil inside the tube.

(2)

Blow across the end of the tube and slide the pencil up and down inside the tube at the same time. You should produce a warbling whistle.

CHAPTER 5
BUSY BODIES

Hands, mouths, and even bottoms have huge potential for making mischief. Whether it is simply being silly or driving people up the wall, all of these ideas deserve a big thumbs-up.

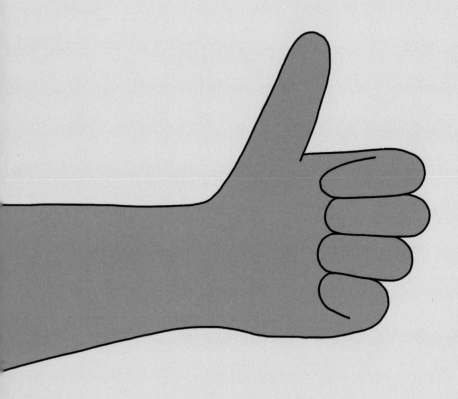

IT'S A HOOT

Use your hands to hoot like an owl.

①

Place your hands together and then twist them in the opposite direction to each other so your fingers create a V-shape.

②

Fold your hands together to make a box shape, with the fingers of your left hand at the back and the fingers of your right hand curving over the top behind your left thumb.

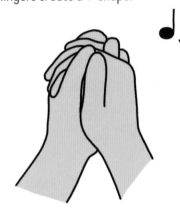

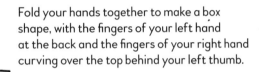

③

Press your thumbs together, then bow them out a tiny bit in the middle to form a gap that opens into the box.

④

Now raise your hands to your mouth. Place your top lip above your thumb knuckles, and your bottom lip below. Blow gently downward over the hole formed by your thumbs. Adjust the angle and the force of your breath until you produce a strong hoot-like noise.

IT'S NO JOKE!

Be careful, the hoot you produce can easily fool owls. In the breeding season, owls hoot to mark their territories, so make sure you don't do it then, or you'll interfere with their breeding. Tu-whit, tu-whoooo!

WIGGLEFINGERS

Can you get giggles with wiggles?

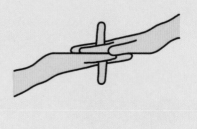

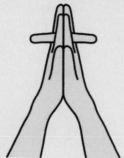

 ①

Place your hands up in front of you, palms pressed together.

 ②

Fold over your middle fingers so they interlock.

 ③

Then rotate your palms in opposite directions.

 ④

It now looks like you have one longer finger going through the center of your hands. Wiggle the fingers in opposite directions for maximum effect. Crowds of thousands can be distracted this way.

TALK TO THE HAND

You will need: • Washable felt-tip pen

Form your hand into a fist with the thumb against your forefinger. Draw two eyes on your forefinger, and a mouth on your thumb with a washable pen. When anyone talks to you, insist that they have to "talk to the hand." Move your thumb up and down in time with your lips. Keep it up for as long as you can!

SHAKEY HANDSHAKE

As you go to shake someone's hand, curl your middle finger up inside your palm and wiggle it against their hand. It's unexpected and feels horrible for them.

EGG ON YOUR
HEAD

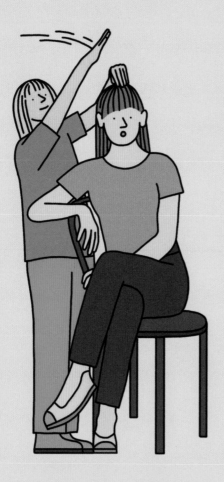

Get someone to sit down and close their eyes while you stand behind them. With one hand, bring your fingertips and thumb together and rest this on their head. Then lightly smack the back of this hand with your other hand to produce a "crack" sound. Now gently spread your fingers across their head. It sounds and feels like someone has cracked an egg on their head!

THUMBS
AWAY

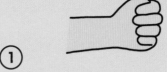

① Tuck one thumb tightly inside your fist.

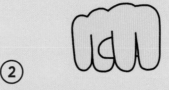

② Fold the other thumb inside your other hand so that the tip sticks out between your middle and ring fingers.

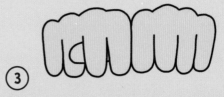

③ Place your fists together so your knuckles are in a row, and it will look like you are holding your own thumb.

④ Pull a face and start making noises as you pull your hands apart and "wrench off" your thumb!

WARNING! If you paint red lipstick onto your "broken" hand, the effect may cause others to faint.

BROKEN NOSE

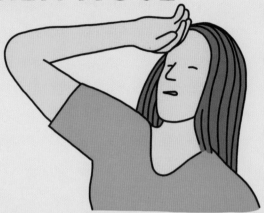 

Cup both hands over your nose and sneakily slip a thumbnail behind your top front teeth. Flip your nail forward as you quickly move your hands to the side. It will look and sound like you're breaking the bridge of your nose!

WARNING! Fainting may, once again, occur.

PULL MY FINGER

With a fart imminent, extend your forefinger and say to a friend: "Pull my finger." As they do so, parp on cue.

Top Tip! Those with excellent fart control can often manage more than one finger pull. Save the little finger for a high-pitched mini-parp.

HAND SHADOWS

Why not stage a shadow battle with your BFFs?

You will need: • Torch

Turn on the torch and shine it at an empty wall. Move your hands in front of the light beam to create a shadow and try out these animals or make some up of your own:

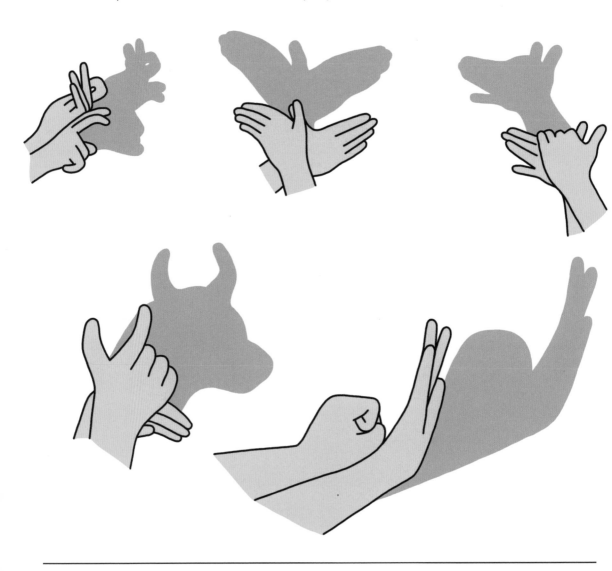

Top tip! You can also hold props such as pens, pencils, and even vegetables. Experiment!

WINDBAG

You will need: • Brown paper bag

Write the words: "DO NOT OPEN!" on the side of a paper bag. Keep it handy for when you can feel a stinky fart coming on. Fart into the bag and quickly fold down the end to close it. Place the bag where any nosey person might dare to open it up. Oh dear...

Top Tip! Disguise your handwriting. If blamed for being the culprit, loudly deny ever dreaming of doing anything so disgusting.

SPOON HANGING

You will need: • Metal spoon

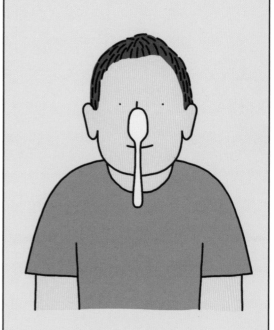

Practice hanging a metal spoon off your nose. One method is to gently drag the bowl of the spoon repeatedly down your nose so it picks up some grease. Or try breathing on the spoon to make it moist.

Top Tip! Great for a contest among your friends at school dinnertime.

IT'S NO JOKE! World records exists for this. One man hung over 30 spoons off his whole face, including his ears.

TONGUE TWISTER

Twist your ear forward with one hand and poke out your tongue at the same time. As you twist your ear back, put your tongue back inside your mouth. Rude and stupid at the same time!

Top tip! Alternatively, twist both ears in turn while moving your tongue from side to side.

THE HUMAN WHALE

Make a loose fist in clean water, then squeeze your fingers closed from the bottom upward to squirt the water. Sploosh!

Top Tip! Can be done in a bowl or sink of water, in the bath, or even in the sea or a swimming pool.

ORANGE PEEL TEETH

After peeling an orange, tear the peel into big scary teeth and pop them under your gums.

BREADSTICK INJURY

To liven up a meal at a restaurant, break a breadstick in to two pieces—one short, one long. Pop the short piece behind your lower lip so that it sticks up. Tuck the longer bit of breadstick under your chin so it looks it you've rammed the whole breadstick through your jaw. Hilarious!

SMART ANSWERS TO
DUMB QUESTIONS

You've probably heard these boring questions a hundred times. Well here are some handy responses that are well worth memorizing.

CHAPTER 6
MAD MAGIC

These tricks will confuse your friends into thinking you are either psychic or a magician. The most important thing is you have to remember how to perform them correctly. Practice helps, plus adopting an air of mystery, as you fool your friends.

LUCKY SEVENS

This trick requires the person whose mind you are reading to use a bit of math, or they can cheat with a calculator.

You will need: • Calculator

1

Ask a friend to think of a number from one to ten. Or one to 100 if they are using a calculator. Tell them not to reveal the number yet!

2

Get them to double the number, then add 12. Next, add five and subtract three.

3

Now get them to divide that new total by two.

4

Finally, ask them to take away the number they first thought of. Pause for a moment and then say, "The total you are now thinking of is seven!" They may be impressed, or fed up with doing math. Either way the answer is always seven.

Top tip! Start the trick by secretly writing the number seven on a blank piece of paper. Hide it away and then tell your friend that their final total will be what is on that piece of paper.

THE BALANCING
EGG

Challenge a friend to balance an egg so it stands vertically on a smooth surface. It is impossible—unless you know how.

Make a small pile of table salt and stand the egg upright on top of it. Now gently blow the salt away with a drinking straw. With just one or two grains of salt remaining, the egg should keep upright.

THE PLAYING CARD
TRICK

Take two playing cards and place one on the floor about 12 inches in front of a friend. Hand them the other card and challenge them to drop it from above their waist so it lands touching the other card.

Most people will hold the card vertically, which means it flutters to one side . On your turn, hold the card horizontally, level with the floor. It should roughly fall in a straight line.

THE COIN ON THE CARD
TRICK

You will need: • Playing card • Coin

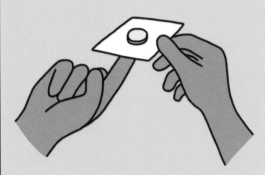

①

Get a friend to extend their forefinger. Balance a playing card on the fingertip and place a coin on top. The trick is to remove the card without the coin falling off. Can they do it?

②

Probably not, but you can! With your hand pull the card away horizontally, quickly. You might want to practice this a few times before you're ready to do the trick perfectly. The card flies off and the coin stays in place. Magic!

THE COIN
SNATCH

You will need: • Lots of coins

Bend your hand toward your shoulder and balance a pile of coins close to your elbow. The trick is to whip your hand over and catch the coins before they hit the floor. It is possible, but without practice there's a big chance of scattering cash all over the place.

IT'S NO JOKE! The coin-snatching world record stands at over 300 coins!

THE COIN CONUNDRUM

A conundrum is a type of puzzle. In this mind-reading trick, the puzzle is for people to work out how you did it. It looks impossible, yet it always works.

You will need: • Six large matching coins, with different dates on them • Plate • At least five friends

① Put your coins on a plate.

② Get together several friends and show them that the coins have different dates on them. Now, while covering your eyes, ask one friend to select a coin at random and, keeping that coin in their hand, put the plate with the remaining coins out of your sight. No one must touch them.

③ Next, explain to your friends that you will read their minds and tell them the date on the chosen coin.

④ Then tell your friends they must each check the date on the coin. They must then pass the coin between them and and press the coin on to their forehead for ten seconds. Say that it is very important that they concentrate on the date. Act super-mysterious. Once everyone has done this the coin can be returned to the plate.

⑤ You need to act quickly now. Pick up each of the coins from the plate and hold them in your hand one at a time, pretending to concentrate. What you are actually doing is feeling which coin is warm. This is the coin that has been held against their heads. The others will be cooler. When you have the warm coin in your hand, read the date out loud. Your friends will be amazed.

Top tip! If you want to get your friends really committed to this trick, offer to let them keep all the coins if you fail to read their minds. It's a pretty safe bet!

THE COIN CONUNDRUM:
PRANK VERSION

Attempt an incredible feat of fakery with this silly prank.

You will need: • Six large matching coins, with different dates on • Paper • Plate • B or 2B pencil

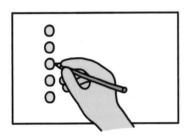

(1) Place five of your coins on a piece of paper and draw around each coin several times with a pencil, so that a thick layer of lead builds up on the edge of each coin. Put the five coins on a plate.

(2) Get together a group of friends and select one, claiming that you feel such a strong mental connection with them that you'd like to try reading their mind.

(3) Take out the sixth—clean—coin from your pocket and, holding it between your fingers so that it can turn like a wheel, run it from side to side across your forehead. Get your friend to practice using the same coin. Tell them: "This is how we do top-level mind reading."

(4) Next, ask them to chose one of the five coins from the plate. To prove that you are not cheating, turn your back and tell them to roll the coin across their forehead and concentrate hard on the date on that coin.

(5) Start pretending that you are trying to connect with their mind. After five seconds or so, proclaim, "I have it!" and turn around.

(6) Guess a date. Any date. It doesn't matter if it is right or not. In fact, it is even funnier if you are wildly wrong. If you are wrong, just shrug and say: "Oh well! Looks like I need to practice more." What your friend won't know—until they look in a mirror—is that they will have drawn a black line across their forehead! If you happen to be with them when they do, run!

COINS IN A ROW

Everyone should know a couple of good coin tricks
—except for the person you're challenging!

You will need: • Six coins, three of one value, three of another

(1)

Place the coins in a row so they alternate.

(2)

Challenge a friend to reorder them (as shown above), so that the coins no longer alternate and the same coins are next to each other. They have to do it in just three moves!

(3)

Here are the rules: they must slide two coins that are next to each other at the same time (they can't swap the position of the coins while sliding them) to wherever there is space (e.g. at either end of the row or, when they've moved the coins, in the space left). Sounds simple? Give it a go yourself, then turn to **page 91** for the solution and commit it to memory!

COINS IN A CIRCLE

A coin-sliding brain teaser.

You will need: • Six matching coins

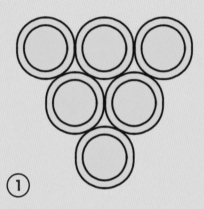

① Arrange the six coins into a triangle.

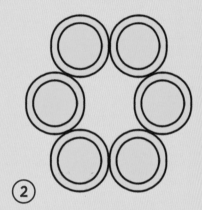

② The challenge is to rearrange them into a circle.

③

The rules are that you can slide only one coin at a time and it must always be touching at least two other coins in its new position. Oh, and you have only four moves!

Did you do it? If not, check the answer on **page 92**, and then challenge everyone you know.

CHAPTER 7
CHAMPION CHALLENGES

No one likes losing, so avoid the possibility by practicing some of these challenges. With these clever tricks, you will always win! Try not to look too eager when asking your "victims" to give them a go, or they'll know you're up to something.

THE HOLE CHALLENGE

Challenge and confuse your friends with this holey hoax.

u will need: • Two circular coins; one should be slightly smaller than the other • Paper • Pencil • Scissors

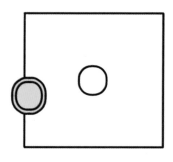

① Draw around the smaller coin on a piece of paper with a pencil. Then carefully cut out the circle to make a hole.

② Tell a friend they can have the coins if they can pass the larger coin through the hole without tearing the paper.

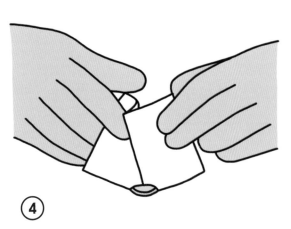

③ When they give up, show them how it is done. Fold the paper across the middle of the hole and drop the larger coin into the folded paper.

④ Then push the edges of the paper inward and pull them apart again. This widens the hole, enabling you to pass the coin through it.

Top tip! Try this challenge with a cookie and a bigger piece of paper. Just be sure to gobble up the cookie before your friend can after it passes through the hole!

THE CHAIR
CHALLENGE

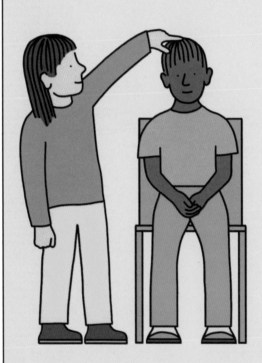

Ask a friend to sit on a chair. Now, placing one finger on top of their head, challenge them to rise to a standing position without leaning forward or using their arms to push themselves up. They can't. It's impossible!

THE WALL
CHALLENGE

Tell a friend to stand with their back to a wall, with their heels touching the wall. Place something lovely—money, candies, a bag of snacks—on the floor in front of them, about 2 feet away or less. Say they can have the treat if they can bend over and pick it up without moving their feet away from the wall. Now watch, as each of their attempts end in failure!

THE PIECE OF PAPER
CHALLENGE

You will need: • A4 paper

Take a piece of paper and make two evenly spaced tears lengthwise, from one edge to the middle. Now challenge a friend to hold the paper at each side and pull it apart so that it ends up in three pieces. They will be guaranteed to fail!

THE SPAGHETTI SNAP
CHALLENGE

You will need: • Spaghetti

Offer someone a million bucks if they can take a piece of ordinary dried spaghetti, and hold it at either end, then bend it and snap in to just two pieces. They can't! The spaghetti always breaks into at least three pieces.

Top Tip! When it is your turn, you can cheat. In advance, ask an adult to use a knife to score a line in the middle of a piece of spaghetti. This will then break in to two pieces.

THE BUCKET OF
WATER CHALLENGE

Definitely best done outdoors, the trick is to have a bucket of water upside down above your head without getting wet.

You will need: • Small bucket with a handle

①

Place a small bucket, full of water, on the ground in front of you. Make sure it isn't too heavy to lift when full. A seaside bucket is perfect. Make sure you're outside.

②

Hold it by the handle and, with your arm extended, swing it quickly in a large circle that goes over your head. You may want to practice a few times first to perfect the trick. The water stays in the bucket because it is constantly being pushed to the sides by the movement.

③

Next, announce that you can sing underwater without a snorkel or any other special apparatus. When they express disbelief, place the bottom of the bucket of water above your head and start singing.

THE BALLOON CHALLENGE

You will need: • Balloon • Pin • Scotch tape

Hand a friend an inflated balloon and a pin. Challenge them to stick a pin in the balloon without making a bang. When they give up, take the balloon, or a new one if they burst it, and put a square of Scotch tape on it. Pierce the balloon through the tape and it won't burst. The tape holds the rubber together, preventing it from exploding.

Top Tip! There is a second version that is tape-free. Simply stick the pin into the unstretched rubber, close to the knot. Air will leak out without the balloon bursting.

THE NEWSPAPER CHALLENGE

You will need: • Newspaper

Hand your friend a sheet of newspaper, and challenge them to produce a straight, vertical tear in it. How you hand the paper to them is important. Newspaper has an invisible "grain," like wood. In most newspapers, the grain runs left to right, so ask your friend to try and tear it from top to bottom. They'll tear it against the grain and the tear will be all jagged. Then you can tear a piece with the grain—and you should get a lovely straight line.

THE HAND
CHALLENGE

Place your hand flat on the top of your head. Challenge a friend to try and lift it off your head by pulling on your forearm. They can't. It's impossible!

THE DOUBLE BOOK
CHALLENGE

You will need: • Two same-sized books

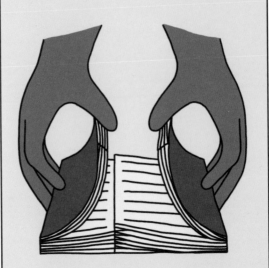

Open up the two books and carefully push them together so that the pages interlock. Close the books and hand them to a friend with the challenge to pull them apart. They can't. It's impossible!

Top Tip! Friction between the pages makes it impossible. To separate the books, you need to get air between their pages once more.

THE ENVELOPE CHALLENGE

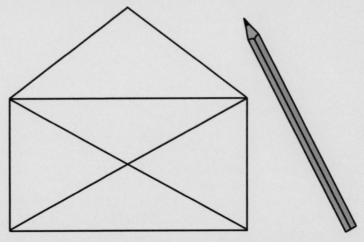

Challenge a friend to draw this envelope, without lifting their pen or pencil off the paper, crossing a line, or going over any line twice. Did they do it? If not, show them the answer on **page 93**.

THE NINE DOTS CHALLENGE

Challenge a friend to connect all nine dots using just four straight lines and without removing their pen or pencil from the paper. Tell them: "Only the most intelligent people can solve this on their own!"

Did they do it? If not, show them the answer on **page 93**.

Top Tip! Tell your friend to try "thinking outside the box."

IT'S NO JOKE! This puzzle was used as an intelligence test for would-be employees of the Walt Disney Corporation.

CRISS-CROSS CHALLENGE

You will need: • Paper • Two different-colored pens • One friend

①

Take the first pen, and draw two crosses an inch or so apart.

②

Now extend one of the "arms" from the first cross to an arm of the second cross. Make a small mark in the middle of the line you have just drawn to create a third arm.

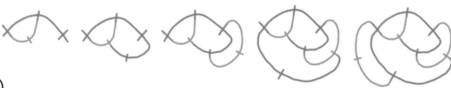

③

Now, using the second pen, get your friend to join two different arms together with a line. They must then add a mark in the middle of the line they have just drawn to make another arm. At this point, stop the demonstration and explain that play continues until no new connections can be made. It could go something like the examples above ...

④

The person who makes the last possible connection is the winner. The final image could look similar to the above picture. Now get ready to start again! Start the next game by drawing two fresh crosses, then hand your friend the pen and challenge them again. To be a guaranteed winner, just remember that if you start with an even number of crosses, you need to go first to win, and if you start with an odd number of crosses, you need to go second.

ANSWERS

COINS IN A ROW CHALLENGE
ANSWER

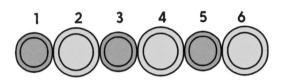

(1)

Imagine the coins are numbered from one to six.

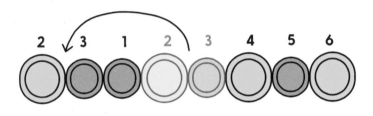

(2)

Take coins two and three and move them in front of coin one.

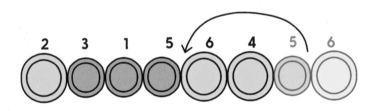

(3)

Take coins five and six and move them to the space created by moving coins two and three in step two.

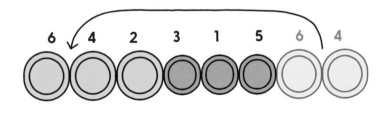

(4)

Finally, take the last two coins in the row, coins six and four, and move them to the front of the row and you've done it!

COINS IN A CIRCLE CHALLENGE
ANSWER

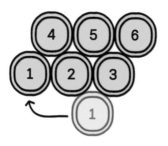

 1

Imagine the coins are numbered from one to six. Now move coin one next to coins two and four so the coins form two lines.

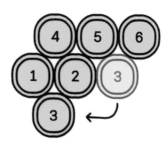

2

Move coin three below coins one and two.

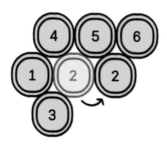

 3

Slide coin two to the right so it sits below coins five and six.

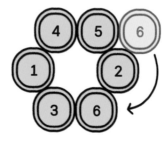

4

Finally, move coin six inbetween coins two and three. And you have a circle!

THE ENVELOPE CHALLENGE
ANSWER

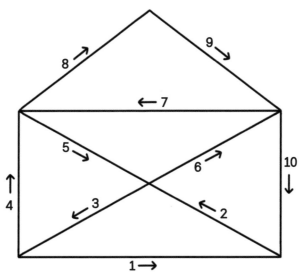

There are lots of ways to complete this image, and here's one version. Put your pen on the paper and follow the above steps, number by number. The arrows show you which way to move your pen.

THE NINE DOTS CHALLENGE
ANSWER

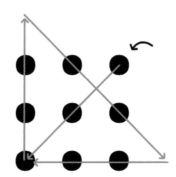

It's a bit tricky, this puzzle. To solve it, you have to imagine the dots form a box, and extend the lines outside it.